BRILLIANT BLACK INVENTORS

written by

Joy James

illustrated by

Karen Dowie

Michael Terence
Publishing

– For Milton, Jade and Jules –

INTRODUCING OUR BRILLIANT BLACK INVENTORS...

LONNIE JOHNSON

Do you like squirting water at bath time?

Lonnie invented the water gun which squirts water!

Lonnie called his toy the Super Soaker water gun
and it's now called the Nerf gun!

It's great for playing water fights outside
in the garden or in the park!

Watch out! You'll all get very wet!

United States Patent

HENRY THOMAS SAMPSON

Henry invented a special rocket fuel that helps rockets zoom to the moon!

Fuel is rocket food!

Hungry rockets need fuel food to launch into space!

Which planet would you like to visit?

CATHERINE WICKS

Do you like to eat crisps?

They were invented by accident!

Catherine was a chef at a restaurant.

One day she was chopping potatoes and a thin slice fell into the pan and got cooked by mistake!

It tasted delicious! Yum yum!

Everybody loved them so she made some more!

Catherine
Crisps
POTATOS
POTATOS

ALEXANDER ASHBOURNE

Alexander was a bit fussy about his biscuits!

In the old days, biscuits were made by hand into funny, odd shapes!

Alexander didn't like this, so he invented biscuit shapes to make good-looking biscuits!

We like animal biscuit shapes the best!

THATO KGATLHANYE

When Thato was still a schoolgirl she invented
a very special school bag!

It can shine a light at night-time
to help you to see in the dark! Magic!

Thato's school bags use recycled plastic bags
and solar energy from the sun to power the light
so they are helping to save our planet too!

WILLIAM SACHITI

William invented a car that drives without a driver!

He called it Kar-go!

Kar-go drives around by itself
and delivers packages to people!

It uses robot technology and artificial intelligence!
Wow, cool stuff!

MADAM CJ WALKER

(Sarah Breedlove)

Looking after your hair is important!

Sarah invented great hair products to keep hair healthy.

Her hair salon business became
very well-known and famous.

Sarah had a very fancy business name -
Madam CJ Walker!

Do you have another name or a nickname?

Shampoo

MOSES FLEETWOOD WALKER

(no relation to Madam CJ Walker!)

Do you like watching films at the cinema?

Moses loved films and worked in a cinema!

In the old days, cinemas used film reels to show films – some still do!

Moses invented ways to improve the way film reels worked.

What's your favourite film?

WILLIAM DAVIS

William was a Buffalo soldier during the American Civil War!

He rode a horse all day long which was rather uncomfortable, so he invented a more comfortable riding saddle! Cowboys loved his invention! Yeehaw!

Have you ever ridden a horse... or a pony... or a llama?

THOMAS ELKINS

What does a fridge do?

Imagine a house without a fridge!

Where would you keep all your fresh food?

Thank goodness for Thomas who invented the fridge!

It helps to keep everything nice and cold
so remember to keep the door shut!

Clever man!

GEORGE BECKET

Imagine not having a letterbox in your front door!
How would the postperson deliver your post?

You might have to wake up early and answer the door
if they had any letters for you – YAWN...!

George's letterbox invention was a very simple idea
but it's a great one!

Do you peep through your letterbox to see what's going
on outside?

GEORGE BECKET
1 THE RED HOUSE
HAPPY VILLAGE
SW3 1PQ

MIRIAM BENJAMIN

Have you pushed the call button above your seat
in an aeroplane?

It's very useful if you need something from the flight
attendant – like a drink, if you're thirsty!

The idea for it came from Miriam's 'gong and signal' chair
invention – you pushed a button at the back
which made a GONG sound and a light lit up
so the attendant could find you!

Amazing!

CHARLES BROOKS

Charles invented a road sweeper –
it was a machine, not a person!

It had whirly round brushes to give the road a proper clean, and scrapers to scrape ice off the ground in the winter, and a dustpan and bin to sweep it all up and away!

Have you ever seen a machine cleaning up the roads?

ROBERT FLEMMING

Can you play a musical instrument — maybe the piano... or the drums... or the recorder?

Robert invented the guitar!

He called it a Euphonica - it was bigger than other string instruments in those days and made a louder sound ...strum, StRuM, STRUM!

Do you like music... or singing... or dancing?

GERALD LAWSON

Gerald's friends called him Jerry.

He invented the first home video game console machine, just like Nintendo and Xbox and PlayStation!

It's fun to play them but it's also fun to play outside with your friends!

What's your favourite game to play inside or outside?

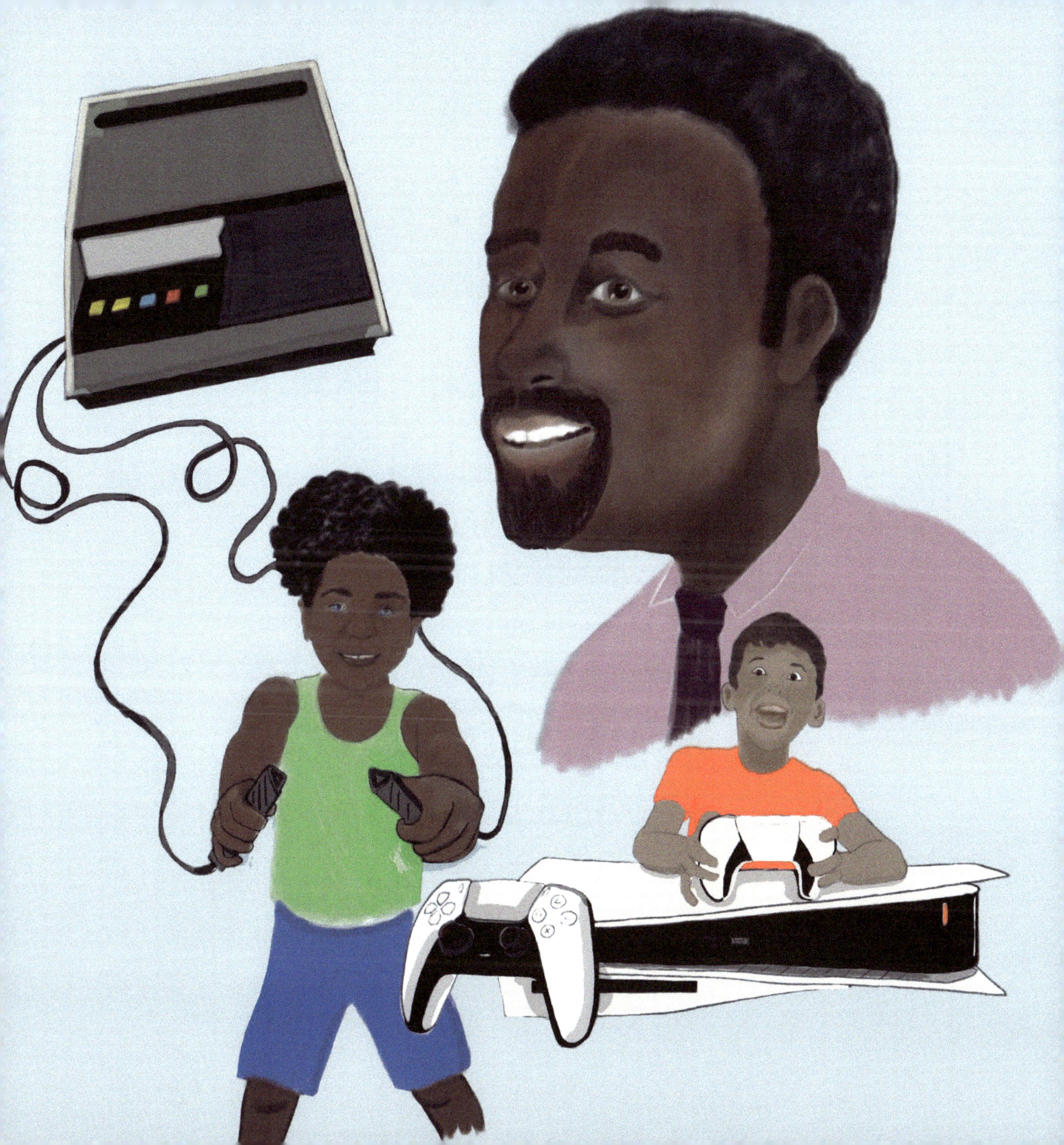

ALICE PARKER

Alice hated feeling cold – BRRR!

Her fireplace couldn't keep her whole house warm enough
so she invented central heating
to make her home feel nice and toasty!

She was a very clever lady!

What do you like best about winter?
We love snow but not the cold too - BRRR!

Acknowledgements

A huge thank you to Karen Dowie for her creative ideas and lovely illustrations.

Grateful thanks to Keith Abbott at Michael Terence Publishing for his advice and help in getting this book published.

Lots of love and thanks to my wonderful family for inspiring and encouraging me on my writing journey.

About the Author

Joy James lives in London with her family. She works at a university and writes non-fiction children's books to help educate and inform curious, young minds.

Her first book, ***101 Black Inventors and their Inventions***, is aimed at upper primary to lower secondary school ages.

Watch out for further books in her ***Black Inventors Series*** aimed at different age groups.

First published in paperback in 2021 by Michael Terence Publishing
www.mtp.agency

ISBN 9781800942424

Illustrated by Karen Dowie

www.ingramcontent.com/pod-product-compliance
Ingram Content Group UK Ltd.
Pitfield, Milton Keynes, MK11 3LW, UK
UKHW061950290726
14090UKWH00021B/1164

9 781800 942424